No part of this publication may be reproduced, stored in a retrieval system, or transmitted in any form or by any means, electronic, mechanical, photocopying, recording, or otherwise, without written permission of the copyright owner.

لا يجوز إعادة إنتاج أي جزء من هذا المنشور أو تخزينه في نظام استرجاع أو نقله بأي شكل أو بأي وسيلة الكترونية أو ميكانيكية أو تصوير أو تسجيل أو غير ذلك دون الحصول على إذن خطي من مالك حقوق الطبع والنشر.

MY MORALS

أَخْلاقِي

Copyright © 2025 by Taymaa Salhah. All rights reserved.

جميع الحقوق محفوظة | تيماء صالحة © ٢٠٢٥

ISBN: 978-1-7751528-6-6

I am a **Muslim**.
I recite the Shahada.

I bear witness that there is no god but Allah, and that Muhammad is the Messenger of Allah.

أَنا مُسْلِمٌ، أَشْهَدُ أَنْ لَا إِلَهَ إِلَّا اللهُ، وأَنَّ مُحَمَّدًا رَسُولُ اللهِ.

I pray five times a day.
أُصَلِّي خَمْسَ صَلَوَاتٍ فِي الْيَوْمِ.

I pay Zakat.

أُؤْتِي الزَّكَاةَ.

I fast during the month of Ramadan.

أَصُومُ شَهْرَ رَمَضَان.

I perform Hajj.

أَحُجُّ بَيْتَ اللهِ.

There's more!
هُنَاكَ الْمَزِيدُ!

I am a Muslim.
I have to be **honest** and **trustworthy**.

أَنا مُسْلِمٌ، يَجِبُ أَنْ أَكُونَ صَادِقًا وأَمِينًا.

I tell the truth, even if I don't like the consequences.

أَقُولُ الْحَقِيقَةَ، حَتَّى لَوْ لَمْ أُحِبَّ الْعَواقِبَ.

{وَالَّذِينَ هُمْ لِأَمَانَاتِهِمْ وَعَهْدِهِمْ رَاعُونَ ۝ وَالَّذِينَ هُم بِشَهَادَاتِهِمْ قَائِمُونَ ۝ وَالَّذِينَ هُمْ عَلَىٰ صَلَاتِهِمْ يُحَافِظُونَ ۝ أُولَٰئِكَ فِي جَنَّاتٍ مُّكْرَمُونَ ۝} [المَعَارِج: ٣٢-٣٥]

"32. ˹The faithful are˺ also those who are true to their trusts and covenants;
33. and who are honest in their testimony;
34. and who are ˹properly˺ observant of their prayers.
35. These will be in Gardens, held in honour."
—The Clear Quran 70:32-35

I don't cheat, even if I love winning.
لا أَغُشُّ، حَتَّى لَوْ أَحْبَبْتُ الْفَوْزَ.

I don't take what isn't mine, even if I really like it.
لا آخُذُ مَا لَيْسَ لِي، حَتَّى لَوْ أَعْجَبَنِي كَثِيرًا.

{وَٱلسَّمَآءَ رَفَعَهَا وَوَضَعَ ٱلْمِيزَانَ ۝ أَلَّا تَطْغَوْا۟ فِى ٱلْمِيزَانِ ۝ وَأَقِيمُوا۟ ٱلْوَزْنَ بِٱلْقِسْطِ وَلَا تُخْسِرُوا۟ ٱلْمِيزَانَ ۝}
[الرَّحْمَٰن: ٧-٩]

"7. As for the sky, He raised it ˹high˺, and set the balance ˹of justice˺
8. so that you do not defraud the scales.
9. Weigh with justice, and do not give short measure."
— The Clear Quran 55: 7-9

I keep my promises, even if it's a lot of work.

أَفِي بِوُعُودِي، حَتَّى لَوْ كَانَ ذَلِكَ يَتَطَلَّبُ الْكَثِيرَ مِنَ العَمَلِ.

﴿وَأَوْفُوا۟ بِعَهْدِ ٱللَّهِ إِذَا عَـٰهَدتُّمْ وَلَا تَنقُضُوا۟ ٱلْأَيْمَـٰنَ بَعْدَ تَوْكِيدِهَا وَقَدْ جَعَلْتُمُ ٱللَّهَ عَلَيْكُمْ كَفِيلًا ۚ إِنَّ ٱللَّهَ يَعْلَمُ مَا تَفْعَلُونَ﴾ [النَّحْل: ٩١]

"91. Honour Allah's covenant when you make a pledge, and do not break your oaths after confirming them, having made Allah your guarantor. Surely Allah knows all you do."
— The Clear Quran 16:91

I am a Muslim.
I have to be **kind** and do **good**.
أَنا مُسْلِمٌ، يَجِبُ أَنْ أَكُونَ مُحْسِنًا.

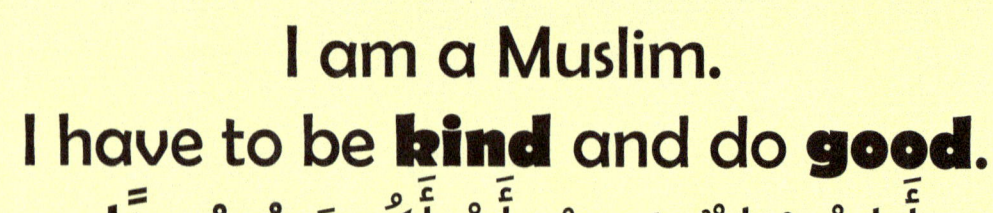

I care about others.
أَهْتَمُّ بِالآخَرِينَ.

I help whenever I can.
أُسَاعِدُ كُلَّمَا اسْتَطَعْتُ.

{مَنْ عَمِلَ صَالِحًا مِّن ذَكَرٍ أَوْ أُنثَىٰ وَهُوَ مُؤْمِنٌ فَلَنُحْيِيَنَّهُ حَيَوٰةً طَيِّبَةً ۖ وَلَنَجْزِيَنَّهُمْ أَجْرَهُم بِأَحْسَنِ مَا كَانُوا۟ يَعْمَلُونَ} [النَّحْل: ٩٧]

"97. Whoever does good, whether male or female, and is a believer, We will surely bless them with a good life, and We will certainly reward them according to the best of their deeds."
— The Clear Quran 16:97

I do not tease or call others hurtful names.
I do not laugh at them or offend them.

لا أَغِيظُ الآخَرِينَ ولا أُنَادِيهِمْ بِأَسْمَاءٍ جَارِحَةٍ.

لا أَسْخَرُ مِنْهُم ولا أُسِيءُ إِلَيهِم.

{يَا أَيُّهَا ٱلَّذِينَ ءَامَنُوا۟ لَا يَسْخَرْ قَوْمٌ مِّن قَوْمٍ عَسَىٰٓ أَن يَكُونُوا۟ خَيْرًا مِّنْهُمْ وَلَا نِسَآءٌ مِّن نِّسَآءٍ عَسَىٰٓ أَن يَكُنَّ خَيْرًا مِّنْهُنَّ ۖ وَلَا تَلْمِزُوٓا۟ أَنفُسَكُمْ وَلَا تَنَابَزُوا۟ بِٱلْأَلْقَٰبِ ۖ بِئْسَ ٱلِٱسْمُ ٱلْفُسُوقُ بَعْدَ ٱلْإِيمَٰنِ ۚ وَمَن لَّمْ يَتُبْ فَأُو۟لَٰٓئِكَ هُمُ ٱلظَّٰلِمُونَ} [الحجرات: ١١]

"11. O believers! Do not let some ˹men˺ ridicule others, they may be better than them, nor let ˹some˺ women ridicule other women, they may be better than them. Do not defame one another, nor call each other by offensive nicknames. How evil it is to act rebelliously after having faith! And whoever does not repent, it is they who are the ˹true˺ wrongdoers."
— The Clear Quran 49:11

I am a Muslim.
I have to be **good to my parents**.
أَنَا مُسْلِمٌ، يَجِبُ أَنْ أَكُونَ بَارًّا بِوالِدَيَّ.

I speak to them politely.
أَتَكَلَّمُ مَعَهُمَا بِأَدَبٍ.

"23. For your Lord has decreed that you worship none but Him. And honour your parents. If one or both of them reach old age in your care, never say to them ˹even˺ 'ugh,' nor yell at them. Rather, address them respectfully. 24. And be humble with them out of mercy, and pray, "My Lord! Be merciful to them as they raised me when I was young.""
— Dr. Mustafa Khattab, The Clear Quran 17:23-24

I listen to them.
أُنْصِتُ لَهُمَا وأُطِيعُهُمَا.

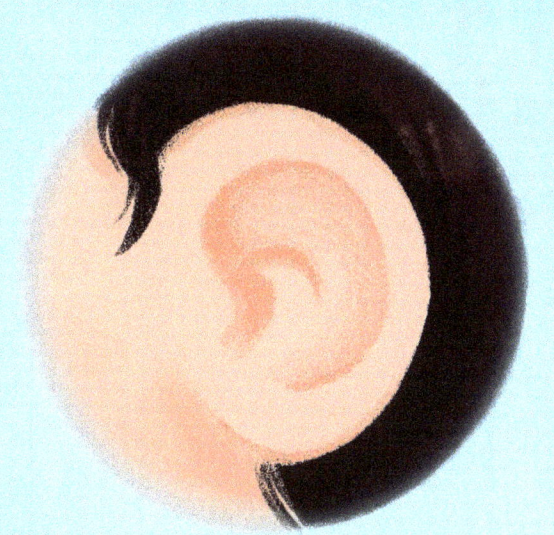

I help them.
أُسَاعِدُهُمَا.

{وَقَضَىٰ رَبُّكَ أَلَّا تَعْبُدُوٓا۟ إِلَّآ إِيَّاهُ وَبِٱلْوَٰلِدَيْنِ إِحْسَٰنًا ۚ إِمَّا يَبْلُغَنَّ عِندَكَ ٱلْكِبَرَ أَحَدُهُمَآ أَوْ كِلَاهُمَا فَلَا تَقُل لَّهُمَآ أُفٍّ وَلَا تَنْهَرْهُمَا وَقُل لَّهُمَا قَوْلًا كَرِيمًا ۝ وَٱخْفِضْ لَهُمَا جَنَاحَ ٱلذُّلِّ مِنَ ٱلرَّحْمَةِ وَقُل رَّبِّ ٱرْحَمْهُمَا كَمَا رَبَّيَانِى صَغِيرًا ۝}
[الإسراء: ٢٣-٢٤]

I am a Muslim. I have to be **fair**.
أَنا مُسْلِمٌ، يَجِبُ أَنْ أَكُونَ **عادِلًا**.

I take turns with my friend.
أَتَناوَبُ مَعَ صَديقي اللَّعِبَ عَلَى الأُرْجوحةِ.

I accept the consequences of my behavior.
أَقْبَلُ عَوَاقِبَ سُلُوكِي.

﴿إِنَّ ٱللَّهَ يَأْمُرُ بِٱلْعَدْلِ وَٱلْإِحْسَٰنِ وَإِيتَآئِ ذِى ٱلْقُرْبَىٰ وَيَنْهَىٰ عَنِ ٱلْفَحْشَآءِ وَٱلْمُنكَرِ وَٱلْبَغْىِ ۚ يَعِظُكُمْ لَعَلَّكُمْ تَذَكَّرُونَ﴾ [النَّحْل: ٩٠]

"90. Indeed, Allah commands justice, grace, as well as generosity to close relatives. He forbids indecency, wickedness, and aggression. He instructs you so perhaps you will be mindful."
— The Clear Quran 16:90

I am a Muslim. I have to be **forgiving**.
أَنا مُسْلِمٌ، يَجِبُ أَنْ أَكُونَ عَفُوًّا.

My secret recipe for FORGIVENESS:

Ingredients: Strength, courage, kindness, and a pinch of wisdom

Step 1: I stand up for myself. I tell my friends how their actions made me feel.

Step 2: I explain to my friends how I like to be treated instead.

Step 3: I forgive.

> I'm sad that you broke my toy. Please be more careful next time. I forgive you.
>
> أَنَا حَزِينٌ لِأَنَّكَ كَسَرْتَ لُعْبَتِي. لَوْ سَمَحْتَ، كُنْ أَكْثَرَ حَذَرًا فِي الْمَرَّاتِ الْقَادِمَةِ. أَنَا أُسَامِحُكَ.

وَصْفَتِي السِّرِّيَّةُ لِلْعَفْوِ

الْمُكَوِّنَات: قُوَّة، شَجَاعَة، إِحْسَان، وَرَشَّة مِنَ الْحِكْمَة

الْخُطْوَةُ الْأُولَى: أُدَافِعُ عَنْ نَفْسِي أَقُولُ لِأَصْدِقَائِي كَيْفَ شَعَرْتُ تِجَاهَ تَصَرُّفِهِم.

الْخُطْوَةُ الثَّانِيَةُ: أَشْرَحُ لَهُم كَيْفَ أُحِبُّ أَنْ يُعَامِلُونِي.

الْخُطْوَةُ الثَّالِثَةُ: أَصْفَحُ عَنْهُم.

﴿وَجَزَٰٓؤُاْ سَيِّئَةٖ سَيِّئَةٞ مِّثْلُهَاۖ فَمَنْ عَفَا وَأَصْلَحَ فَأَجْرُهُۥ عَلَى ٱللَّهِۚ إِنَّهُۥ لَا يُحِبُّ ٱلظَّٰلِمِينَ﴾ [الشورى: ٤٠]

"40. The reward of an evil deed is its equivalent. But whoever pardons and seeks reconciliation, then their reward is with Allah. He certainly does not like the wrongdoers."
— The Clear Quran 42:40

I am a Muslim. I have to be **patient**.
أَنا مُسْلِمٌ، يَجِبُ أَنْ أَكُونَ صَابِرًا.

I wait for my turn to speak.
أَنْتَظِرُ دَوْرِي لِأَتَكَلَّم.

I wait for my turn to play.
أَنْتَظِرُ دَوْرِي لِأَلْعَبَ.

Good things are worth waiting for!
الْأَشْيَاءُ الْجَيِّدَةُ تَسْتَحِقُّ الْإِنْتِظَارَ!

﴿إِلَّا ٱلَّذِينَ صَبَرُواْ وَعَمِلُواْ ٱلصَّٰلِحَٰتِ أُوْلَٰٓئِكَ لَهُم مَّغْفِرَةٌ وَأَجْرٌ كَبِيرٌ﴾ [هُود: ١١]

"11. except those who patiently endure and do good. It is they who will have forgiveness and a mighty reward."
— The Clear Quran 11:11

I am a Muslim. I have to be **tolerant**.
أَنا مُسْلِمٌ، يَجِبُ أَنْ أَكُونَ **مُتَسَامِحًا**.

I respect everyone no matter how different we may be.

أَحْتَرِمُ الْجَمِيعَ مَهْمَا كُنَّا مُخْتَلِفِين.

I am a Muslim. I have to **control my anger**.
أَنا مُسْلِمٌ، يَجِبُ أَنْ أَتَحَكَّمَ في غَضَبي.

I do not hit. I do not yell. I do not say bad words or hurtful things.

I take a deeeeeep breath. I sometimes count down to calm myself.

Then I use my words to express my feelings and stand up for myself.

"134. They are˹ those who donate in prosperity and adversity, control their anger, and pardon others. And Allah loves the good-doers."
— The Clear Quran 3:134

لَا أَضرِبُ، لَا أَصرُخُ، ولَا أَقُولُ كَلِمَاتٍ بَذِيئَةٍ أَو جَارِحَةٍ.

آخُذُ نَفَسًا عَمِييييييقًا وَأَقُومُ أَحْيَانًا بِالْعَدِّ التَّنَازُلِيِّ لِتَهْدِئَةِ نَفْسِي.

ثُمَّ أَسْتَخْدِمُ كَلِمَاتِي لِلتَّعْبِيرِ عَنْ مَشَاعِرِي وَالدِّفَاعِ عَنْ نَفْسِي.

﴿الَّذِينَ يُنفِقُونَ فِي السَّرَّاءِ وَالضَّرَّاءِ وَالْكَاظِمِينَ الْغَيْظَ وَالْعَافِينَ عَنِ النَّاسِ ۗ وَاللَّهُ يُحِبُّ الْمُحْسِنِينَ﴾ [آلِ عِمْرَان: ١٣٤]

And there is a lot more!
وَهُنَاكَ الْمَزِيْدُ!

So, what good can I do today?
فَما الْخَيْرُ الَّذِي يُمْكِنُنِي أَنْ أَفْعَلَهُ الْيَوْمَ؟

www.ingramcontent.com/pod-product-compliance
Lightning Source LLC
Chambersburg PA
CBHW061116070526
44583CB00027B/3316